RHINOCEROSES

IVING WILD

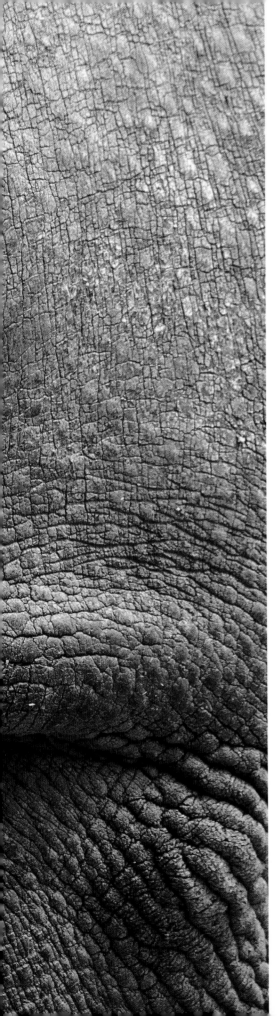

LIVING WILD

Published by Creative Education
P.O. Box 227, Mankato, Minnesota 56002
Creative Education is an imprint of The Creative Company
www.thecreativecompany.us

Design and production by Mary Herrmann
Art direction by Rita Marshall
Printed by Corporate Graphics in the United States of America

Photographs by 123RF (Chris Kruger), Alamy (AllOver Photography, Chris George, Steve Bloom Images, Ann and Steve Toon, Tom Uhlman, Robert M. Vera, David Wall, WorldFoto), Alain Compost, Corbis (Annie Griffiths Belt, Petr Josek/Reuters), Dreamstime (Martina Berg, Mikhail Blajenov, Oleg Blazhyievskyi, Sascha Burkard, Odelia Cohen, Elizabeth Hammerschmid, Jeremyrichards, Mpetersheim, S100apm, Samrat35, Trouvail, Keith Wheatley, Judy Worley), Getty Images (Beverly Joubert, Pietro Longhi, Nicholas Parfitt, Mary Plage, Joel Sartore, Superstock), iStockphoto (Hilton Kotze, Grigory Kubatyan, David Long, Peter Malsbury, mddphoto, Pauline S Mills, Birger Niss, Irving N Saperstein, Sohl, Sandra Vom Stein)

Library of Congress Cataloging-in-Publication Data
Gish, Melissa.
Rhinoceroses / by Melissa Gish.
p. cm. — (Living wild)
Includes bibliographical references and index.
Summary: A look at rhinoceroses, including their habitats, physical characteristics such as their horned noses, behaviors, relationships with humans, and protected status in the world today.
ISBN 978-1-60818-083-7
1. Rhinoceroses—Juvenile literature. I. Title.

QL737.U63G57 2011
599.66'8—dc22   2010028316

CPSIA: 110310 PO1385

First Edition
9 8 7 6 5 4 3 2 1

 CREATIVE EDUCATION

RHINOCEROSES

Melissa Gish

A female black rhinoceros ambles through the
tall, dry grass, following the scent of something

unseen. It is a warm, sunny winter afternoon

in South Africa's Pongola Game Reserve.

A female black rhinoceros ambles through the tall, dry grass, following the scent of something unseen. It is a warm, sunny winter afternoon in South Africa's Pongola Game Reserve. But it is the second month with no rainfall, and the earth is parched and cracked. The rhino travels for several miles until the ground slopes downward slightly and the grass parts around a small, muddy pool. The rhino steps into the pool, lowers her body, and then rolls over onto her back. Rotating from side to side, she coats her body with a layer of mud that will harden and help keep her cool and her skin conditioned. A male rhino breaks through the grass and silently regards her as she calmly continues her mud bath. Then the male closes his eyes to doze in the sun, content to wait his turn to wallow in the mud.

WHERE IN THE WORLD THEY LIVE

Black Rhinoceros
Kenya, Tanzania, Zimbabwe, South Africa, Swaziland

White Rhinoceros
Namibia, Botswana, Zimbabwe, South Africa

Indian Rhinoceros
India and Nepal

Javan Rhinoceros
Java

Sumatran Rhinoceros
Malaysia, Sumatra, Borneo

Of the five rhinoceros species, the two African varieties can be broken down further into subspecies, according to geographical location. The three Asian rhinos, though, are more limited to distinct parts of the world. The colored squares represent common locations of each species living in the wild today.

REMARKABLE RHINOS

Rhinoceroses and elephants, two of Africa's most well-known animals, share habitats on that continent.

T he rhinoceros is the second-largest land **mammal** in the world, behind the elephants of Africa and Asia and ahead of the African hippopotamus. Of the five rhinoceros species, the tallest is the Indian rhino of Asia, which can stand about six and a half feet (2 m) tall at the shoulder. The white rhino of Africa, though the same weight as the Indian rhino, is about six inches (15 cm) shorter, and both the African black rhino and the Javan rhino of Asia are about six inches (15 cm) shorter still. The smallest rhinoceros species is the Sumatran rhino, which stands just over four and a half feet (1.4 m) tall at the shoulder. Male rhinos are typically 10 to 20 percent heavier than females. Male Sumatran rhinos average about 1,700 pounds (711 kg), but male white rhinos can top 7,000 pounds (3,175 kg).

Rhinoceroses belong to the family Rhinocerotidae. The word "rhinoceros" comes from the Greek words *rhin*, meaning "nose," and *keras*, meaning "horn." Rhinos are members of the order Perissodactyla, a group of animals with an odd number of toes on each foot. Rhinos and their closest relatives, tapirs, have three toes. The middle toe is

Although rhinos and tapirs have three toes, they are still classified as hoofed animals known as ungulates.

Fewer than 50 Javan rhinos exist in their last refuges, Indonesia's Ujung Kulon National Park and Vietnam's Cat Tien National Park.

slightly longer than the other toes and carries the bulk of the animal's weight. Other members of this order include horses, asses, and zebras, which have just one toe—the hoof—on each foot.

Rhino habitats include grasslands, forests, and lowland rainforests, where these massive animals can find all the food they need for their vegetarian diets. Indian rhinos are found in India and Nepal, in the forested foothills of the Himalayas. This species has just one horn, but the single horn can grow to be up to four and a half feet (1.4 m) long and, like those of its African relatives, is highly prized by some native people for its supposed magical properties. The critically endangered Sumatran rhinoceros has 2 horns— 1 above its nose that grows up to 31 inches (79 cm) long and another behind the nose that is usually just a stub. Once widespread throughout Asia, the Sumatran rhino is now found only in southern mainland Malaysia and on its islands of Sumatra and Borneo. The rarest of all large mammals on Earth is the Javan rhinoceros, hunted to near **extinction** for its single 10-inch (25.4 cm) horn. It exists only on the island of Java and in a Vietnamese national park.

There are two subspecies of white rhino: northern

The gravely endangered Javan rhino
is also known as the Sunda rhinoceros
and the lesser one-horned rhinoceros.

Rhinos typically follow trails established by elephants that connect foraging grounds to watering holes.

and southern. Garamba National Park in the Democratic Republic of the Congo was the last refuge of the northern white rhino, but in recent years, **poachers** killed the few that remained, leaving this subspecies extinct in the wild. Only eight northern white rhinos were housed in zoos around the world as of 2010, and two of these lived in San Diego, California. In contrast, southern white rhinos are the most plentiful, numbering about 17,000 in population, and are found in scattered pockets across Namibia, Botswana, Zimbabwe, and South Africa. They live on flat savannas, where they graze on up to 90 pounds (41 kg) of grasses each day.

The critically endangered black rhinoceros shares some of its habitat with the southern white rhino. The four distinct subspecies of black rhino are divided by geography. Eastern black rhinos are found in Kenya and Tanzania. South-central black rhinos are found mainly in Zambia and South Africa. Southwestern black rhinos are found in Namibia, South Africa, and Zimbabwe. Western black rhinos, the last of which were likely poached from their final refuge in Cameroon between 2008 and 2010, share the fate of northern white rhinos: extinction. Worse yet,

The black rhino has a **prehensile** upper lip that it uses like a finger to grab vegetation and push it into its mouth.

The shoulders of the white rhinoceros feature the thickest skin on its body; it can be up to 1.7 inches (4.3 cm) thick.

there are no western black rhinos in captivity; these animals are now gone from the planet forever.

The rhinoceros is an incredibly powerful animal. It has thick bones and large muscles in its legs and can run up to 28 miles (45 km) per hour in short bursts. The strong muscles in its shoulders and neck support its heavy head. The skull has a thick bump where the horn is anchored. The horn is not part of the skull, so if it breaks off, the horn can grow back. Horns are made of keratin, the same material found in human fingernails, but are thicker than nails— similar in density to cow hooves. The white rhino's horn can grow to be six feet (1.8 m) long. A rhino's horn is sometimes used for defense, especially during mating season when males fight over females, but horns are mostly used for tearing up vegetation and digging watering holes. The black rhino uses its horn to break down tree limbs so it can eat the leaves.

Rhinos have 12 to 14 pairs of square molars in the back of their jaws designed for grinding up food. Their teeth **evolved** to match the animals' varying diets. African rhinos have tiny front teeth that are virtually useless, as these rhinos rely on their molars to grind up the grass on which they graze. Because their diet is much different, Asian

In the dry season, rhinos must often cross one another's territories in search of water, which can lead to fights.

Mother rhinos will often step on foliage to bend it down to a suitable height for their young to reach.

rhinos have sharp incisors used for shearing off vegetation from bushes and tree branches.

A rhino's thick layer of skin is actually rather soft. In fact, the skin around its snout is as velvety as a horse's snout. Asian rhinos have more pronounced skin folds and bumps than African rhinos do. Rhinos like to wallow in mud, coating their bodies with a protective layer of natural sunblock and skin conditioner. Their ears are trimmed with hair, and the tail has stiff bristles of hair. But apart from the red-haired Sumatran rhino, no other rhinos have much hair covering their bodies.

Rhinoceroses have excellent hearing and a strong sense of smell. Their eyesight is very poor, though. For this reason, rhinos have unfairly earned a reputation as aggressive animals. Because they cannot see objects clearly from a distance, they may charge forward, looking as though they mean to fight, when in reality they are just trying to protect themselves or their young from potential harm. They may charge anything from other animals and people in vehicles to stationary objects such as trees and rocks. Despite its large size, the rhinoceros has a relatively small brain and typically reacts before it reasons.

The Sumatran rhino, with its long, woolly hair, has survived virtually unchanged over millions of years.

The rhino relies on smell to get around, and its system of scent organs and nasal passages is larger than its brain.

with her again to keep other bulls away from her. The cow carries her single calf for 15 to 16 months, one of the longest **gestation** periods of any mammal. Then she gives birth while standing up.

Indian and white rhinos are the largest newborn rhino calves. They average 2 feet long (0.6 m) and weigh up to 100 pounds (45 kg). At 55 to 75 pounds (25–34 kg), newborn Sumatran and Javan rhinos are the smallest. A newborn calf is mentally alert and can stand within an hour of its birth. For the first three to five years of its life, a young rhino is dependent on its mother for emotional

and physical security. When it is relatively small, a
calf is vulnerable to attack by lions, tigers, hyenas, and
crocodiles. The mother rhino must remain constantly
alert to such dangers.

Calves live on their mother's milk for the first several
months. Then they begin eating grass like their mother.
Eventually, milk becomes only a minor part of a calf's diet,
and it will stop nursing when its mother becomes pregnant
again, which can occur every two or three years. When it is
fully grown and no longer needs protection, a young rhino
will wander away from its mother and begin life on its own.

Rhinos forage for food in the early morning and then again at dusk and later into the night. During the hottest parts of the day, they seek out shade from the sun, water for drinking, and mud for wallowing. Rhinos roll around in mud to coat their bodies with the cooling substance whenever it is available. The Asian rhino species usually have no problem locating water in their rainforest habitats, but in Africa, finding water can be a challenge. During the dry season, which occurs sometime from early spring to late fall—depending on the region—rhinos may need to travel for days to find water. While rhinos prefer to drink every day, they can go up to six days without water if they feed mostly on grasses and leaves, which contain more moisture than bushes and twigs.

The rhinoceros is an herbivore, meaning it eats only vegetation. Its strong lips tear grasses and strip leaves from branches. White rhinos common to the African bushveld—a subtropical woodland area in southern Africa where thorny bushes and acacia trees grow—are grazers that use their strong, flat lips to rip up grass. However, Africa's black rhino and the three species of tropical rainforest rhinos—all featuring curved lips—are browsers.

African rhinos will drink between 15 and 25 gallons (57–95 l) of water each day whenever it is readily available.

Oxpeckers generally eat ticks and other insects but also use their thick beaks to pick at scabs on rhinos' skin.

They pull apart herbs and shrubs and strip twigs and leaves from the branches of small trees.

The African rhinos have special relationships with certain birds that share their grassy habitats. The cattle egret—also called the rhinoceros egret—is a slender white bird with long legs that follows moving rhinos, feeding on the ground-dwelling insects that are disturbed by the rhinos' grazing. The 20-inch-tall (51 cm) birds are completely fearless of the hulking rhinos. In 2000, researchers in South Africa reported seeing a cattle egret with an injured leg riding on the back of a mother rhino who was grazing with her calf. The bird would occasionally float to the ground to snatch insects and then fly back up to the rhino's back for a ride. The rhino, despite being naturally protective of her calf, did not seem to consider the bird a threat.

Another bird that provides a service to rhinos in exchange for riding piggyback is the oxpecker, also known as the tickbird. The oxpecker is a grayish-brown-colored bird that is slightly smaller than a robin. One species has a red beak, the other a yellow beak. They ride large mammals that roam the African grasslands—

including rhinos—eating **parasites** off the animals' hides. They also eat the tiny insects that invade wounds in animal flesh, which helps speed the healing process. While some animals, such as elephants, refuse to tolerate oxpeckers, rhinos allow these birds to clean every inch of their bodies—including their faces.

Rhinos play an important role in their **ecosystems**. They tear up vegetation and grassland, encouraging new growth, and their dung is useful in spreading seeds from place to place and providing built-in fertilizer for the new plants and trees that spring from those seeds.

Rhinos kick up insects as they move, making it easy for such small birds as cattle egrets to obtain food.

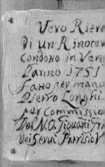

In the 1700s, Italian artist Pietro Longhi depicted Europeans' fascination with a rhino named Clara.

ROUGH AND TOUGH RHINOS

The rhinoceros may have received a bad name for being grumpy in the wild, but rhinos **adapt** well to captivity. Many early rulers—from as far back as the Roman emperors of more than 2,000 years ago—kept them in **menageries** and sent rhinos and other exotic animals to one another to build their collections and promote friendship. In 1515, a ruler in southwest India sent a rhino, along with its keeper, to the king of Portugal. No one living in Europe had ever seen a live rhinoceros before, so the event caused a great stir. When the Belém Tower was constructed in Lisbon (between 1515 and 1521), it was decorated with the image of a rhinoceros—the first sculpture of the animal to appear in western European art.

To find out which animal was more fearsome—and believing the two were enemies—the Portuguese king arranged a battle between the rhino and an elephant from his collection. The rhino was not interested in fighting, and the elephant ran away in fear of the noisy crowd. Perhaps disappointed with the calm demeanor of the rhino, the king decided to give it away. He sent it to

White rhinos are less territorial and aggressive than black rhinos, which are not social animals.

About half of black rhino males and one-third of black rhino females who fight die from combat wounds.

Pope Leo X in Rome, but the ship that carried it sank in a storm off the coast of northern Italy.

Word of the rhinoceros had reached German artist Albrecht Dürer within weeks of the rhino's arrival in Portugal. He created a woodcut based solely on a written description and simple sketch given to him by a man who had seen the rhino in Portugal. Dürer's woodcut was not scientifically accurate; nonetheless, it became one of the most famous images of a rhinoceros ever created. Rhinos appeared only a few times in Europe over the next 200 years, but when they did, they made a big impression.

Before Jean-Baptiste Lamarck and Charles Darwin proposed their theories of natural evolution, French naturalist Georges-Louis Leclerc, Comte de Buffon, proposed many ideas that ran counter to the traditional teachings of the history of the Earth and the existence of life forms. Before his death in 1788, Buffon, known as the founder of **biogeography**, published 36 volumes of his *Histoire Naturelle*, in which he described and illustrated many plants and animals—including an Indian rhinoceros named Clara, who toured Europe in the mid-18th century.

A Dutch trader working in India raised Clara as a

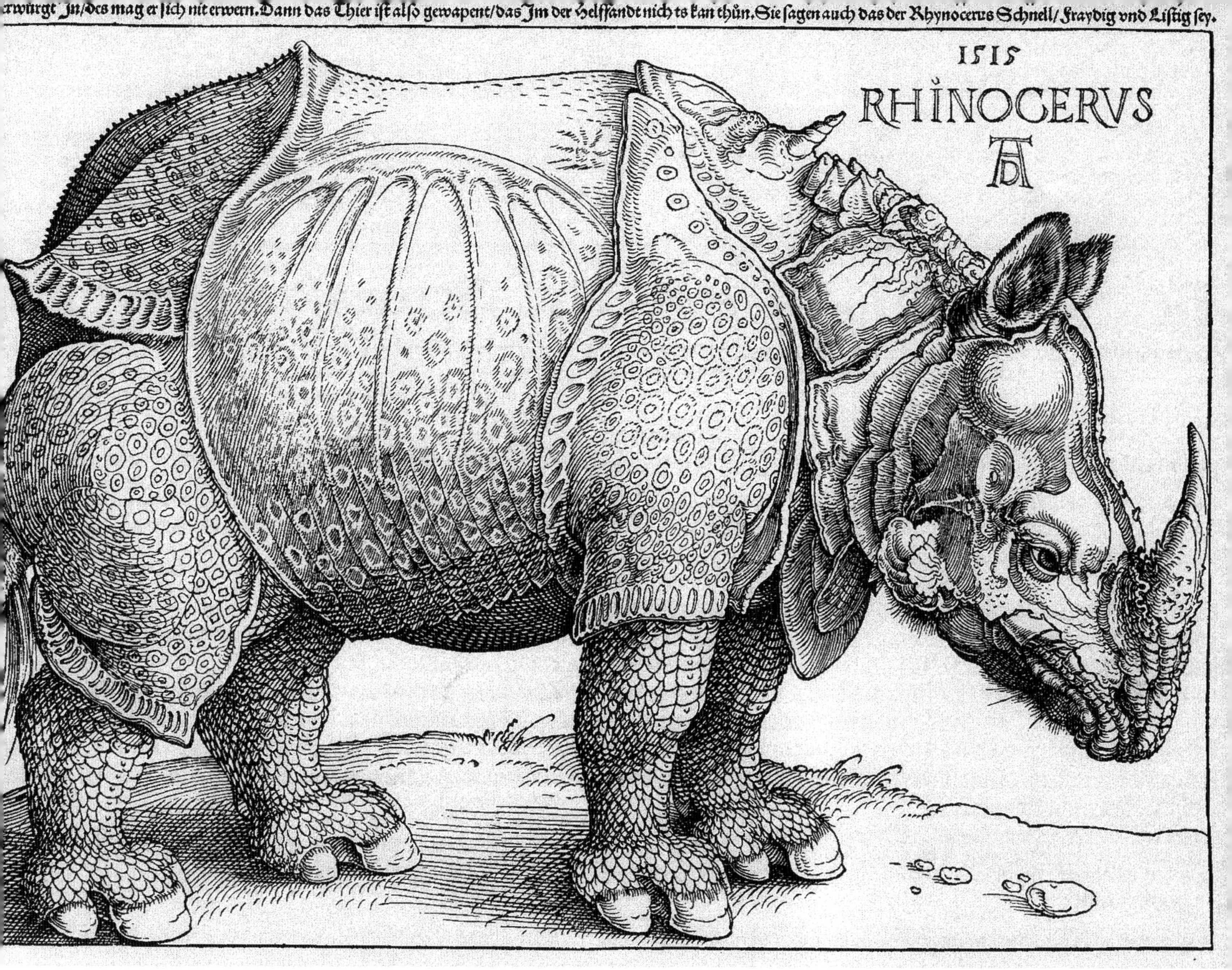
erwürgt Jn/des mag er sich nit erwern. Dann das Thier ist also gewapent/das Jm der Helffandt nichts kan thůn. Sie sagen auch das der Rhynocerus Schnell/Fraydig vnd Listig sey.
1515
RHINOCERVS

pet after she was orphaned as an infant. When she was nearly three years old, Clara was sent to the Netherlands, where she was put on public display. For more than 17 years, she traveled throughout Europe, and people loved her so much that they wrote songs and poems about her. Clara was nearly 21 years old and weighed 3,000 pounds

Albrecht Dürer's woodcut provided a model for such artwork as paintings, porcelain figures, and bronze statues.

Conservation workers sometimes remove rhino horns to deter poachers, but it is still distressing to the animal.

Because rhinos are such large animals, poachers routinely use machine guns to shoot them and chainsaws to remove their horns.

(1,361 kg) when she died in London in 1758.

Another captive rhinoceros that made headlines around the world more recently was Emi, a Sumatran rhinoceros loaned to the Cincinnati Zoo from the government of Indonesia. When Emi and her male counterpart, Ipuh, arrived in the United States in 1996, they became the first Sumatran rhinos in captivity in North America. Emi was also famous for being the first Sumatran rhino to successfully give birth in captivity in more than 100 years and the only Sumatran rhino to successfully give birth 3 times.

The 2007 book *Emi and the Rhino Scientist*, by Mary Kay Carson, tells the fascinating story of Emi and her keepers at the Cincinnati Zoo, which hosted more than 1.2 million visitors per year during the time Emi was in residence. Unfortunately, Emi suffered liver failure in 2009 and died, but her three offspring were all healthy as of 2010 and provided scientists with vital information about their species that may help save the Sumatran rhino from extinction.

While Emi and her offspring were making news around the world, two rhino-like mammals were making people laugh. When Blue Sky Studios and 20th

Emi the rhino and her babies raised money for the Cincinnati Zoo by painting pictures with their prehensile lips.

Salvador Dali believed the rhinoceros horn was a perfect example of the mathematical structure of nature.

Century Fox released the animated film *Ice Age* in 2002, Frank and Carl, a pair of brontops—prehistoric rhino relatives—got as many laughs as the film's star sloth and mammoth did. Despite their gruff personalities, Frank and Carl were not true rhinos, as brontops were more closely linked to horses.

As big as prehistoric rhinoceros relatives were, they would have been no match for one of Europe's most famous pieces of art. Inspired by Dürer's 1515 woodcut, the renowned Spanish artist Salvador Dali created a massive sculpture called *Rinoceronte vestido con puntillas* (*Rhinoceros Dressed in Lace*), in 1956. On display in Marbella, Spain, the bronze sculpture weighs nearly four tons (3.6 t) and wears armored plating, as is shown in Dürer's drawing, with Dali's added touch of lacy designs.

While some rhinoceroses, such as the Indian rhino, look as though they have plates of armor, they do not. Still, rhinos have a reputation for being tough. Several military machines have been nicknamed "Rhino" as a symbol of strength, such as the F/A-18F Super Hornet fighter plane, which was first used by the U.S. Navy in 1999. The Super Hornet is considered to be a very tough airplane and is the envy of many air forces around the world. In fact, the Royal Australian Air Force ordered its entire fleet of fighter planes to be replaced with the Rhino in 2007.

The Rhino Runner is a heavily armored, custom-built bus that has been used extensively by the U.S. military and others in Iraq. Strongly protected against bomb blasts and completely impervious to bullets on all sides, including the undercarriage and windows, the Rhino Runner is considered one of the toughest and most reliable vehicles in use today.

The rhino's fierce reputation makes it the perfect inspiration for one of the comic book world's most aggressive supervillians: the Rhino. First appearing in *The Amazing Spider-Man* comic series in 1966, the armored Rhino sports a razor-sharp horn and boasts superhuman strength and stamina. On the more playful side, a purple rhinoceros is the star of the popular family game Rhino Rampage, in which players try to get all of their birds safely on the rhino's back before the rhino rumbles, throwing off the birds. From great art to fun games, the rhinoceros is a unique creature that has captivated people's imaginations for hundreds of years.

An F/A-18F Super Hornet costs more than $60 million to build, due to the craft's complex electronics and weapons.

Paleontologists are scientists who study prehistoric life, including rhino fossils that date back millions of years.

POISED ON THE BRINK

Male rhino beetles use their horns against each other when sparring over mating rights.

The earliest rhinoceros ancestors had bodies like modern rhinos, but they did not have horns. Instead, they had tusks that grew from the lower jaw. About 50 million years ago, some of the largest rhinoceros ancestors, such as the *Hyracodontidae*, also known as "running rhinos," stood as tall as giraffes. Early rhinos were mostly concentrated in Asia, but about 10 million years ago, some species migrated to Africa. Over the next five million years, various species and subspecies of rhino evolved.

The woolly rhinoceroses (*Coelodonta antiquitatis*), which roamed Europe during an ice age (a period when ice sheets covered much of Earth) of about 23,000 years ago, most closely resembled modern rhinos. Their remains were first discovered in Poland in 1929. The flesh and organs of the animal had been soaked in salt and mineral oil in the swamp in which it had been trapped, so the **carcass** was naturally **mummified**. The specimen was stuffed and exhibited at the Muzeum Przyrodnicze (Museum of Natural History) in Krakow, Poland, where it can still be seen today.

The five rhino species descended from the woolly rhino may be unofficially subdivided further according

The rhinoceros beetle, named for the rhino-like horn on its head, is one of the strongest insects in the world.

Ecotourism, which allows people to visit rhino habitats in Africa, India, and Southeast Asia, helps fund rhino conservation efforts.

to geography. In 2000, scientist and veterinarian Annelisa Kilbourn, working with a nonprofit organization called SOS Rhino, established a program in the Tabin Wildlife Reserve on the Malaysian island of Borneo to track a unique subspecies of Sumatran rhino. *Dicerorhinus sumatrensis harrissoni*, or the eastern Sumatran rhinoceros, is found only in the northern Bornean state of Sabah. SOS Rhino has reported that only about 25 of these rhinos, which are smaller than the regular Sumatran rhino, still exist. To keep track of rhino populations, researchers use **satellite** photography, **Global Positioning System** (GPS) tracking equipment, and remote-controlled cameras. Getting visual confirmation of rhinos is extremely difficult, so scientists must often trek through the rainforest to search for evidence of rhino activity, such as mud wallows or footprints.

The rhinos in the Tabin Reserve, which covers roughly 475 square miles (1,230 sq km), are isolated by mangrove swamps and palm plantations. The expanding palm oil industry in Indonesia and Malaysia is blamed for major **deforestation** in the areas where Sumatran and Javan rhinos struggle to survive.

NATURAL-BORN ENEMIES

At the same games the rhinoceros was also exhibited, an animal which has a single horn projecting from the nose; it has been frequently seen since then. This too is another natural-born enemy of the elephant. It prepares itself for the combat by sharpening its horn against the rocks; and in fighting directs it chiefly towards the belly of its adversary, which it knows to be the softest part. The two animals are of equal length, but the legs of the rhinoceros are much the shorter: its skin is the color of boxwood.

Pliny the Elder (A.D. 23–79), excerpt from Natural History

Researchers prefer to airlift rhinos instead of driving them when moving the animals to breeding programs.

Habitat fragmentation can trap rhinos in lowland areas, causing them to drown during seasonal floods in Southeast Asia.

Habitat fragmentation is one of the major problems plaguing rhinos throughout Asia as well as northern Africa. When rhinos are separated from one another by human development and industry, they are less able to mate or are forced to mate repeatedly with rhinos in their immediate area. This inbreeding weakens the **gene** pool and can lead to the extinction of rhinos in that area.

Research on the problems associated with a lack of genetic variety has been conducted in Gorumara National Park in northeast India. The small park of about 31 square miles (80 sq km) is home to about 35 Indian rhinos, which are closely monitored by park officials and conservation experts. In recent years, the rhino population has increased slightly due to greater attention being paid to the problem of poaching, but the park holds more males than females, which has affected the ultimate mating success of these animals.

Similar issues with gender imbalance are seen in game reserves and national parks all across Asia and northern Africa. To address this problem, government agencies and park officials from various countries participate in translocation programs, moving rhinos from one place to another in efforts to strengthen the gene pools in certain areas. The land in and around Dudhwa National Park, located on the border of India and Nepal, was once insufficient to contain the overflow of Indian rhinos in the region, but the rhinos were then hunted to extinction there. In an attempt to reintroduce the species to the area, conservationists worked with the Indian government to create the Rhino Rehabilitation Program, which began in 1984 with five rhinos moved to Dudhwa from another national park. The following year, 5 more rhinos were moved, and today, Dudhwa is once again home to a population of Indian rhinos—about 30 in all.

Captive-breeding programs for wild animals have been established in zoos around the world to help combat the problems associated with inbreeding. But the captive breeding of rhinos has its own set of troubles. Mating rhinos can be aggressive and unruly, making their transport between zoos and their reaction to new housing situations unpredictable and dangerous. Also, rhinos are selective in their mating, and there are no guarantees that two captive rhinos will choose to mate. Even if they do mate, rhinos under the stress of captivity rarely conceive offspring.

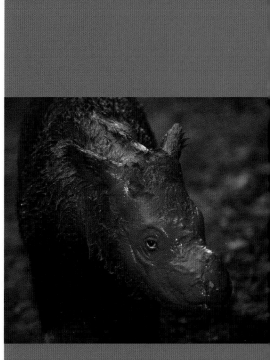

Because more than 50 percent of captured Sumatran rhinos die within a few years, captive breeding could be more harmful than it's worth.

Bibi, a black rhino at the Sedgwick County Zoo in Wichita, Kansas, mated with her zoo-mate Eugene several times, but none of the **fetuses** developed, and Bibi was unable to have a calf for many years. Finally, aided by zoo staff and veterinarians, Bibi delivered a healthy male calf in 1993. Such successes are few and far between. The next time a black rhino birthed a calf in North America was at Louisiana's Baton Rouge Zoo in 2009.

Rhinos were wiped out of the East African country of Uganda by 1982, but the Ziwa Rhino Sanctuary, established in 2002, translocated four white rhinos from Kenya in 2005 in an effort to reintroduce the species in Uganda. In 2006, Disney's Animal Kingdom in Florida donated two more rhinos to the sanctuary. By the end of 2009, two calves had been born there, and three other females were pregnant. Conservationists have agreed that Ziwa is one of translocation's greatest success stories.

Despite continued efforts to increase their numbers, rhinos are still poised on the brink of extinction. The greatest threat to rhino populations is poaching, which has increased in recent years. Demand for rhino horn as an ingredient in some traditional Chinese remedies is

also responsible for driving some poorer people in places such as Nepal, Zimbabwe, and South Africa to risk breaking the law to sell it in order to feed their families. It is unfortunate that rhinos must suffer the consequences of the economic crises of the world. Tireless efforts by conservationists and scientists, however, may yet preserve the rhinoceros for future generations.

Rhinos are being wiped out in Zimbabwe, where poaching doubled in 2009 to support the growing Chinese black market.

ANIMAL TALE: THE ORIGIN OF THE SUMATRAN RHINO

The Sumatran rhinoceros is the smallest of the five rhino species and the only one with a visibly hairy coat. This folk story from Malaysia explains how the Sumatran rhinoceros came to exist.

Long ago, a giantess named Gedembai appeared in Malaysia. She had wild, red hair and a huge lump on the top of her nose. She had evil magic in her words, too. If she said to someone, "You look like a goat!" that person would change into a goat. And if she cast a certain spell, a person could be turned instantly to stone. All the people feared her, and when she declared herself queen of all the land, she forced the people to do everything she commanded or face the punishment.

The people obeyed Gedembai, giving her the best crops and hunting the biggest game for her. They built her a huge house on a mountaintop that overlooked the sea. They learned that appearing weak and never looking Gedembai in the eyes would keep them safe from her wrath. They did everything Gedembai commanded, but silently they prayed to the *Na Tuk Kong*, or guardian spirits, to send someone to help them drive her away.

Gedembai punished the people day after day. Finally, the village elders held a secret council to discuss how they might be able to get rid of her. But nothing could be kept secret from the giantess, who had the power to see what people were doing, even from far away. Gedembai stormed the council chambers and turned all of the village elders to stone. Then she climbed up the mountain and stood atop her mansion, screaming in anger at the people's scheming.

The *Na Tuk Kong* heard Gedembai's screams and decided that she had been selfish and cruel for long enough. They sent a prince with a magical dagger to help the people. The prince appeared before Gedembai and told her that she must either stop being selfish and cruel to the people or leave. Gedembai laughed at the prince and spoke the magic words to turn him into stone. But the prince did not turn into stone. Instead, he took a step closer to Gedembai and raised his dagger.

Gedembai, angered at the prince's defiance, spoke the words again. Nothing happened. "You look like a goat!" she cried. But the prince did not turn into a goat. "You look like a snake!" she cried. But the prince did not turn into a snake. With each curse that Gedembai spoke, the prince took another step closer to her. Finally, standing before her, he plunged the dagger into Gedembai's heart and said, "You look like *badak api*!"

Instantly, Gedembai ignited into a blazing inferno. She stomped her feet to make the flames die down, but then Gedembai found that she had been transformed into a strange animal with a horn on the top of her nose. Her flesh had turned dark brown, and she was left with only thin patches of reddish hair. She was so horrified of what she had become that she ran away into the jungle, becoming frightened and shy, and has remained in hiding ever since as the Sumatran rhino, or *badak api*, the rhinoceros on fire.

GLOSSARY

adapt – change to improve its chances of survival in its environment

biogeography – the study of where organisms are distributed and how many occur in a particular place

captive-breeding – bred and raised in a place from which escape is not possible

carcass – the dead body of an animal

deforestation – the clearing away of trees from a forest

ecosystems – communities of organisms that live together in environments

evolved – gradually developed into a new form

extinction – the act or process of becoming extinct; coming to an end or dying out

fetuses – the unborn offspring of mammals that have all their features (limbs, organs, eyes, etc.) and a basic resemblance to the adult

gene – the basic physical unit of heredity

gestation – the period of time it takes a baby to develop inside its mother's womb

Global Positioning System – a system of satellites, computers, and other electronic devices that work together to determine the location of objects or living things that carry a trackable device

mammal – a warm-blooded animal that has a backbone and hair or fur, gives birth to live young, and produces milk to feed its young

menageries – collections of wild or unique animals that are kept on display

mummified – when a body has been preserved from decay by natural conditions such as extreme cold, bogs, or salt, or by being filled and covered with plants, minerals, and oils

parasites – animals or plants that live on or inside another living thing (called a host) while giving nothing back to the host; some parasites cause disease or even death

poachers – people who hunt protected species of wild animals, even though doing so is against the law

prehensile – capable of grasping

satellite – a mechanical device launched into space; it may be designed to travel around Earth or toward other planets or the sun

SELECTED BIBLIOGRAPHY

Carson, Mary Kay. *Emi and the Rhino Scientist*. Boston: Houghton Mifflin, 2007.

Cunningham, Carol, and Joel Berger. *Horn of Darkness: Rhinos on the Edge*. New York: Oxford University Press, 2000.

Ellis, Richard. *Tiger Bone & Rhino Horn: The Destruction of Wildlife for Traditional Chinese Medicine*. Washington, D.C.: Island Press, 2005.

International Rhino Foundation. "Homepage." http://www.rhinos-irf.org.

Mishra, Hemanta. *The Soul of the Rhino*. Guilford, Conn.: Lyons Press, 2009.

Saving Rhinos. "Homepage." http://www .savingrhinos.org/index.html.

Rhino calves rely on their mothers for protection, but as they grow, their mothers teach them to defend themselves.

INDEX